Bats, Butterflies, and Bugs

Bats,
Butterflies,
and Bugs

A Book of Action Toys

S. ADAMS SULLIVAN

Little, Brown and Company

BOSTON   TORONTO   LONDON

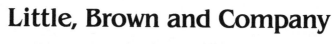

For Greg, Rita, and Tim —
a bat, a butterfly, and a bug.

First Edition

10 9 8 7 6 5 4 3 2 1

BP

*Published simultaneously in Canada
by Little, Brown & Company (Canada) Limited*

PRINTED IN THE UNITED STATES OF AMERICA

Library of Congress Cataloging-in-Publication Data

Sullivan, St. Clair Adams.
    Bats, butterflies, and bugs / S. Adams
Sullivan. — 1st ed.
    p.   cm.
    Summary: Instructions for making a variety of
toys which look like bugs, butterflies, or bats.
    ISBN 0-316-82185-3 : $12.95
    1. Handicraft — Juvenile literature.   2. Bats —
Juvenile literature.
3. Insects — Juvenile literature.   [1. Toy
making.   2. Handicraft.
3. Bats — Miscellanea.   4. Insects —
Miscellanea.]   I. Title.
TT157.S848   1990
745.592 — dc20   89-39792
                                                                CIP
                                                                AC

Contents

Introduction 7
Copying Full-size Patterns 8

Toys, Treats, and Thrills

Instant Bat Wings and Quick Bat Ears 10
Spinning Butterflower 12
Cuddly Bedbug 14

Mini Piñata Bat 18
Butterfly Marionette 20
Motor Bug Roach Coach 24

A Bat in Your Hat 26
Circling Butterflies 28
Giant Attack Bug 30

Batburgers 32
High-Climb Butterfly 34
Stink Bugs and Perfume Bugs 36

Magnetic Bat 38
Butterfly Twirler 40
Wind-up Water Bug 44

Helicopter Toys

Whirly Bat 48
Buttercopter 50
Bug Chopper 53

Gliders

Bat Glider 56
Butterfly Glider 60
Fly-a-Fly Bug Glider 64

Kites

Dracula's Bat Kite 68
Butterfly on a Magic Wand 72
Easy Bug Kite 76
Kite-Flying Tips 79

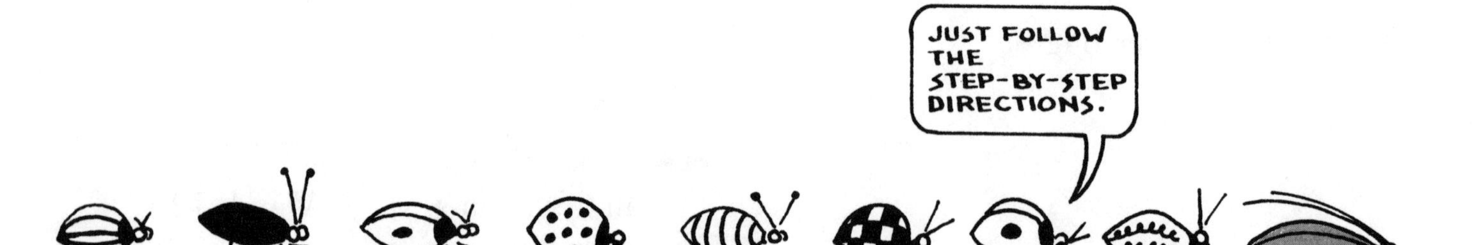
JUST FOLLOW THE STEP-BY-STEP DIRECTIONS.

Introduction

Kids! Get ready to build some super action toys that fly, float, flutter, spin, swirl, glide, and race around the room. They look and act like bats, butterflies, and bugs.

You won't find these toys at the mall. They're extra fun because you build them yourself. When you make your own toys, you can say, "Hey, Toys 'Я' Me!"

Follow the step-by-step directions, and you'll find that building the toys will be fast and easy. Most take less than half an hour.

The materials you need are all things you have at home or can easily buy in a variety store — like construction paper, index cards, paper clips, and cellophane tape.

You will need some tools, too: scissors, pencil, ruler, compass, and a black pen.

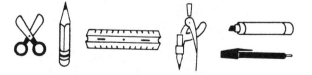

The materials and tools for each project are listed before the step-by-step directions.

Copying Full-size Patterns

Be Your Own Scribble-Power Copy Machine

Many of the toy-building projects in this book have full-size patterns that need to be copied onto construction paper or some other material. Here's an easy, fun way to do it.

You Need:
    1 sheet of tracing paper OR typing paper
    1 pencil

1. Lay a sheet of tracing paper over the full-size pattern in the book. (Or use thin typing paper that you can see through.) Trace the outline of the pattern with a pencil.

2. Turn your piece of paper over and scribble all over the back of the outline with the side of your pencil lead.

3. Lay your piece of paper, scribble side down, on the construction paper or other material. Go over the outline with your pencil, pressing hard.

4. Lift the paper and find a copy of the outline on the construction paper or other material. The pencil scribbles work just like carbon paper.

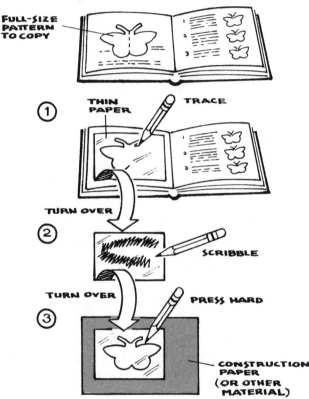

Toys,
Treats,
and Thrills

Instant Bat Wings

Get the feel of flying without leaving the ground. These easy-to-make trash bag Bat Wings gather the breeze as you run and flap.

You Need:
1 black plastic lawn and leaf bag
OR trash bag
Tools: scissors

1. Use the biggest and strongest black plastic bag you can find. One quick scissors cut will turn it into Instant Bat Wings. Start at the middle of the closed end of the bag. Make the cut as long as the distance from your collar to your belt.

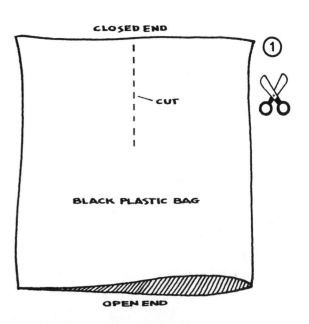

2. Put your arms into the wings pretty much the way you would put on a coat. One at a time your hands go inside the bag at the top of the cut you have made. Push them outward till they end up inside the closed corners of the bag. You can poke your fingers and thumbs through the plastic if you like.

3. Run and flap. But remember — NO jumping off high places. These wings are just for fun.

10

And Quick Bat Ears

Make a stylish pair of Bat Ears to go with your trash bag wings.

You Need:
1 piece of black construction paper (9″ × 12″)
cellophane tape
Tools: ruler, pencil, scissors

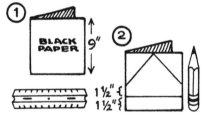

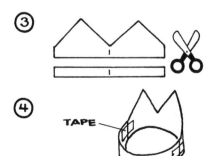

1. Fold a piece of black construction paper so the short sides meet.

2. Use a ruler and pencil to draw the pattern in Diagram 2 onto the construction paper.

3. Cut on the lines through both sides of the paper and open up the two pieces you have made.

4. Tape the pieces together to make a crown. Fit it to your head as you make it.

11

Spinning Butterflower

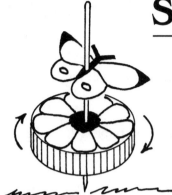

As the top spins, the whirling butterfly seems to hover over the whirling flower. A twist of the fingers sets this little toy twirling. It's easy to make in a few minutes.

You Need:
    small pieces of colored paper
    1 plastic milk bottle cap
    1 toothpick (round OR flat)
    white glue
    Tools: pencil, ruler, black pen, compass

1. Fold a small piece of colored paper and draw on it a half butterfly shape with the centerline of the body along the fold. Make the distance from the fold to the wing tip ¾".

2. Cut through both sides of the paper at once along the outline. Decorate your butterfly shape with a black pen.

① ← ¾" →

COLORED PAPER

②

3. Now make the flower. With a compass, draw a circle on colored paper about the same size as the top of the plastic milk bottle cap. Cut it out. With a black pen, draw petals and a center on it.

4. With the point of your compass, punch a hole in the center of the milk bottle cap. Do this carefully. The closer you get to the exact center, the better your top will spin. Also make a very small compass-point hole in the center of the butterfly.

5. Push a toothpick through the hole in the milk bottle cap so the point is ¼″ below the bottom of the bottle cap. It should fit very snugly in the plastic.

6. Push the top of the toothpick through the holes in the flower and the butterfly. Put the butterfly about ¾″ above the flower. Add drops of glue.

Fancy Footwork on Flowers

Next time you see a butterfly on a flower, sneak up on it quietly from the side and watch what it is doing. Don't come from behind and above or the butterfly will think you're an enemy bird and will fly away.

Watch the butterfly's rear two feet move on the flower. They are probably testing the flower to see if it tastes good. That's right, the butterfly *tastes with his feet*. Where we have toes, he has tiny tarsi that do the tasting.

If kids had their taste buds on their toes, eating ice cream would be even nicer than it already is. And think how much fun you would have eating Jell-O or spaghetti!

If the flower tastes good to the butterfly's feet, he unrolls his long, tubelike tongue, called a proboscis, and uses it like a soda straw to drink the sweet nectar from the flower.

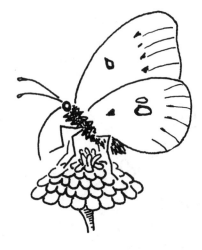

Cuddly Bedbug

A huggable, buggable bedtime pal. Sew the Cuddly Bedbug by hand or on a machine. This is an easy stuffed animal sewing project.

Use any cloth scraps you have. Striped material is best, because a real bedbug has stripes. Brown is a good color for the felt legs and head, with red for the felt eyes, but choose other colors if you like them better. Your bedbug should be beautiful and lovable.

You Need:
> 1 bread and butter dish (about 6½″ across)
> 1 sheet of any paper
> 2 pieces of cloth, 7″ × 7″
> 2 pieces of felt, 6″ × 6″
>   (different colors)
> polyester fiber stuffing
> 1 sheet of tracing paper
>   OR typing paper
> white glue
> *Tools:* pencil, compass,
>   straight pins, scissors,
>   needle and thread
>   OR sewing machine

TAKE THIS BUG INTO YOUR BED
AND INTO YOUR HEART.

14

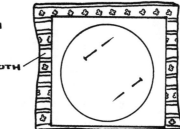

① BUTTER DISH

CLOTH

PAPER

② ✂

CUT TWO

1. Place the bread and butter dish (about 6½" across) upside down on paper and trace its outline with pencil. This is the pattern for the bedbug's body. (If you don't have a 6½" dish, draw a circle pattern with a compass.)

2. Pin the paper pattern to your cloth and cut paper and cloth together. Use the paper pattern to cut a second cloth circle.

3. Cut six strips of felt for legs. Make each strip ½" by 4".

4. Lay one of the cloth circles good side up on a table. Arrange the strips of felt on it this way:

5. Sew the ends of the felt to the edges of the cloth circle about ¼" from the edge.

6. Gather the free ends of the legs in the center of the circle.

7. Lay the second cloth circle, good side down, over the first circle and the bunched legs. Sew the circles together ½" in from their edges. Don't sew the short space between the front legs closed — the head fits in there.

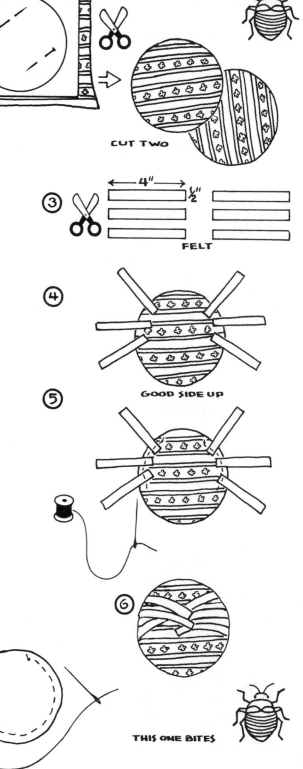

③ ✂ |← 4" →| ½ FELT

④ GOOD SIDE UP

⑤

⑥

A REAL BEDBUG

⑦ GOOD SIDE DOWN

THIS ONE BITES

8. Turn the bug body right side out and stuff it with polyester fiber.

9. Trace the full-size head and antennae pattern on this page on tracing paper or typing paper. Pin the pattern to a piece of felt and cut the paper and felt together.

10. Sewing the head to the body is a little tricky. You may want to get a grown-up to help with this. First, tuck the cloth on one side of the opening down and in to make a straight line between the front legs. Put the base of the felt head inside the opening and sew it to the side you tucked down.

11. Tuck in the cloth on the other side of the opening and sew it to the base of the head.

12. Cut eyes from a different color of felt and glue them onto the head with white glue.

BeanBug or BasketBug

Stuff a Cuddly Bedbug with dry beans instead of polyester fiber and you have a great BeanBug for tossing.

Throw your Cuddly Bedbug or your BeanBug through a hoop and you have a BasketBug.

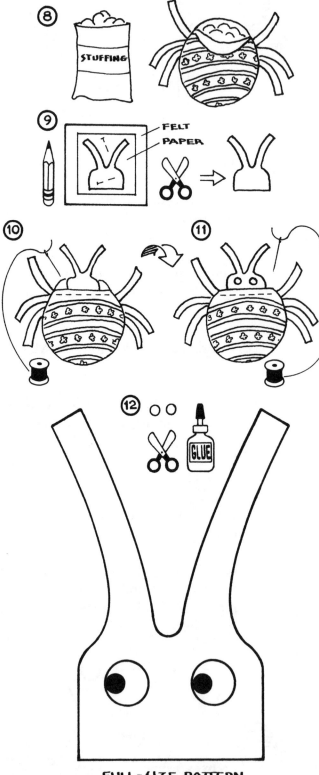

FULL-SIZE PATTERN

Bedbugs, Bats, and Cavemen

Many thousands of years ago people lived in caves — and so did bats. The bats hung from the ceiling and the people lived on the floor, so they didn't get in each other's way very much. They were both happy to share the caves.

Then the people started to itch at night, and they started to scratch. They itched and scratched and scratched and itched till they could hardly stand it. They were being bitten by little bugs that looked just like the bedbugs of today.

At about the same time, the bats began to feel itchy, too. They squirmed and wiggled as they hung from the ceilings of the caves.

One day a caveman was watching a very squirmy bat, and he had an idea. "The bugs must be jumping down on us from the bats," he thought. "If we move out of this cave we won't have to scratch anymore." So the people moved out of the cave and built shelters of sticks and leaves. Later other people learned to build mud huts, and then came wooden houses, and then great mansions, and castles, and cities with tall apartment buildings. But no matter where the people moved or how fine they made their houses, the little bugs followed them. To this day bedbugs still sometimes get into beds and make people itch and scratch and scratch and itch till they can hardly stand it.

Also to this day, bats have little bugs just like bedbugs living on them.

Many people still blame the cave bats for the bedbugs. But the bats tell a different story. Talk to any bat and he will tell you that the *people* brought the darn bugs into the caves in the first place and that the bugs crawled up the walls of the caves from the people to the bats.

This all happened so long ago that no one will ever know the real truth, except maybe the bedbugs, and they aren't talking.

Mini Piñata Bat

Swat the piñata bat with a broom. Smack it as hard as you can. It's perfect for a Halloween party. Make two or three so everyone will get a chance to swing at a bat.

You Need:
 1 sheet of tracing paper OR typing paper
 2 sheets of black construction paper
 cellophane tape
 glue stick OR white glue
 1 paper clip
 black sewing thread
 candy OR healthy treats in wrappers
 1 blindfold
 1 clean broom
 Tools: scissors, pencil, ruler, black pen

Rules:
Blindfold and turn each swatter around three times. You get as many swats as you need to connect. Then the blindfold and broom go to a new swatter.

1. Use the full-size bat pattern for Dracula's Bat Kite on page 71. Follow Steps 1, 2, and 3 on page 8 to cut out the bat shape from black construction paper.

2. With a ruler and pencil, draw a 3½″ × 6″ rectangle on black construction paper. Cut it out and roll it the way Diagram 2 shows.

3. Overlap the ends of the rectangle about ½″ and tape them together to make a cylinder-shape body for the bat.

4. Pinch one end of the cylinder together and tape it shut.

5. Spread glue on the side of the body with the taped seam. Glue the body to the back (valley-fold side) of the bat shape, with the open end up by the head. The wings will be swept back in a realistic bat shape.

6. Cut out and glue on small white circles of paper for eyes. Dot them with a pen.

7. Clip a paper clip to the top back edge of the body and tape it securely in place on both sides of the paper. Tie a 3′ piece of black sewing thread to the paper clip.

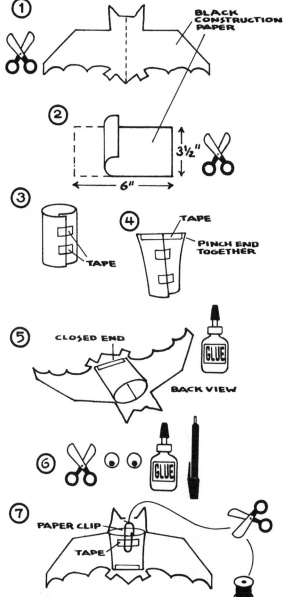

8. Stuff the body with *wrapped* candy or healthy treats. Close the top with crumpled black paper stuffed in and taped down, or leave it open so the candies will fly and scatter when the bat is hit.

9. Get a grown-up to help hang the Bat Piñata over a clear place. A garage doorway is great, or take the piñata outdoors and hang it from a tree branch.

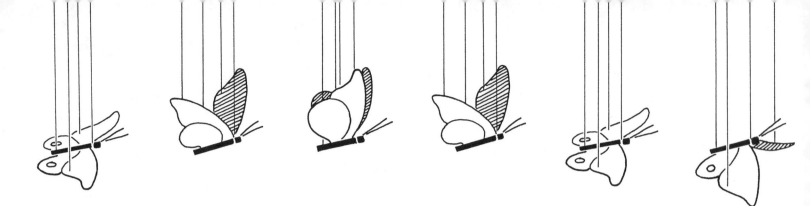

Butterfly Marionette

The Butterfly Marionette moves its wings just like a real butterfly in flight. You can make it fly across the room or hover over a flower pretending to sip nectar. You might even want to give it a part in a play with other marionettes or puppets.

Easy to make if you're good at tying knots.

You Need:
>   1 spring-loaded wooden clothespin
>   white glue
>   1 white 5″ × 8″ index card
>   1 piece of tracing paper OR typing paper
>   black and colored markers
>   black sewing thread
>   2 plastic soda straws
>   cellophane tape
>   *Tools:* pencil, scissors, ruler, compass

1. A spring-loaded clothespin makes the marionette's body. Pull it apart and glue the flat surfaces of the clothespin together.

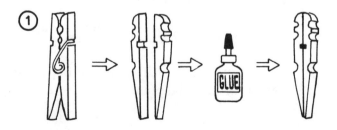

20

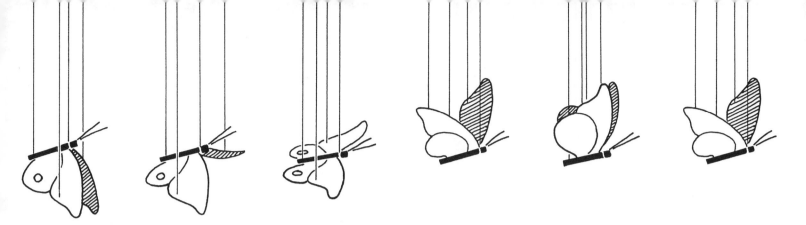

2. Fold a 5″ × 8″ white index card so the short sides meet.

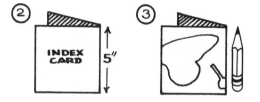

3. Page 8 shows you an easy way to copy the full-size patterns onto the index card. The straight edge of the wing pattern should lie along the *open* end of the card, and the centerline of the head/antennae piece should lie along the *fold* of the card.

4. Cut through both sides of the card at once along the outlines to make two wings and the head/antennae piece.

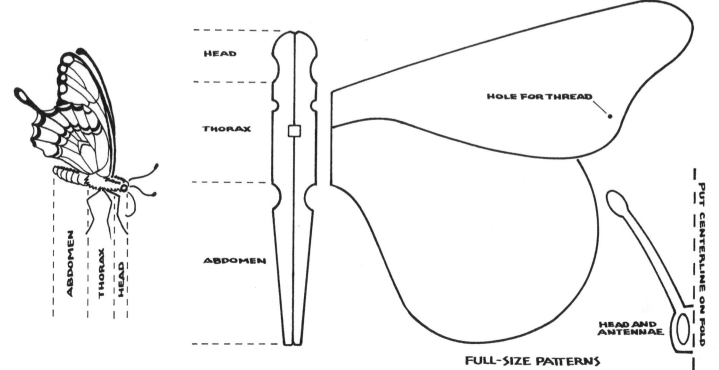

HEAD

THORAX

ABDOMEN

ABDOMEN THORAX HEAD

HOLE FOR THREAD

PUT CENTERLINE ON FOLD

HEAD AND ANTENNAE

FULL-SIZE PATTERNS

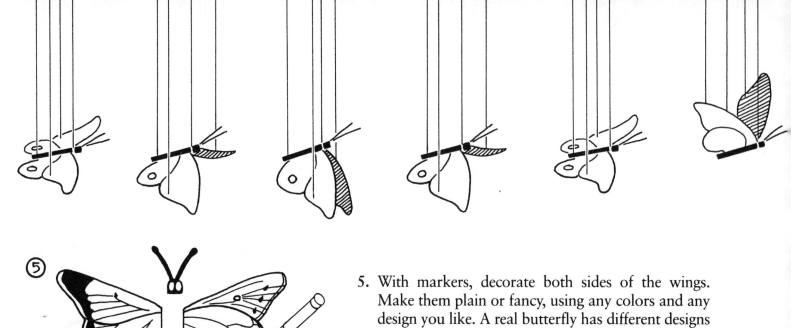

5. With markers, decorate both sides of the wings. Make them plain or fancy, using any colors and any design you like. A real butterfly has different designs on the top and bottom of its wings. You may want to copy a real butterfly design from a book or from a real butterfly. Color the antennae black and draw eyes on the head of the Butterfly Marionette.

6. Cut a strip of paper ½" wide and 2" long. Fold it in half so the long sides meet and then crease it. Now cut it in half to make two hinges.

7. Glue the hinges to the bottom sides of the wings and to the flat sides of the clothespin behind the head section. A real butterfly has three sections to its body: a head, a thorax, and an abdomen. All the muscles that operate the wings are in the thorax, and the wings are attached to this section, so we attach the wings of the marionette to the thorax of the clothespin body.

8. Glue the head/antennae piece to the head section of the clothespin.

9. When the glue is dry, use a black marker to color the whole body black.

TOP   BOTTOM

2″

½″

PAPER

GLUE   THORAX   HINGE

BOTTOM OF WING

GLUE

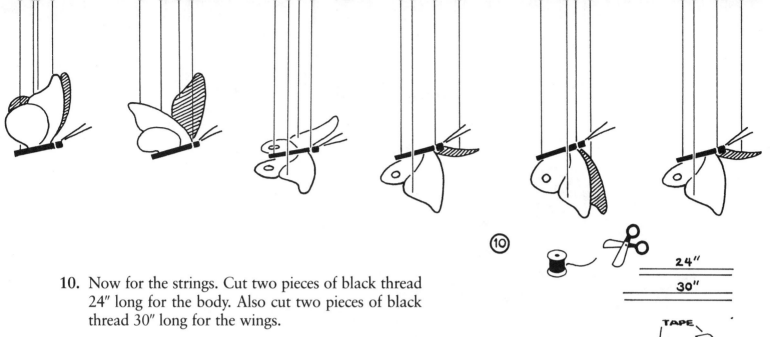

10. Now for the strings. Cut two pieces of black thread 24″ long for the body. Also cut two pieces of black thread 30″ long for the wings.

11. Tie an end of one of the 24″ threads tightly around the groove in the body between the thorax and the head. Tie an end of the other 24″ thread tightly around the groove between the thorax and the abdomen. Tie the free end of each thread tightly around one end of a plastic soda straw. Use a small piece of tape to hold each thread in place on the straw.

12. With the point of a compass, punch holes in the wings at the point shown on the full-size pattern. Tie an end of each 30″ thread through one of these holes. Tie the free end of each thread tightly around one end of a plastic soda straw. Use a small piece of tape to hold each thread in place on the straw.

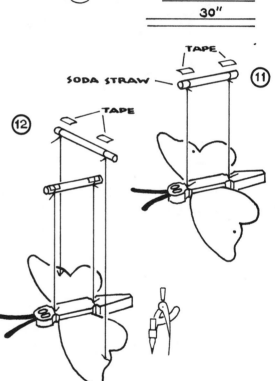

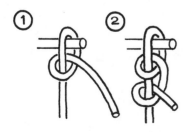

A Good Knot

Here is your best bet for all the knots in the Butterfly Marionette. It's called two half hitches. This is a very easy knot to learn, and you'll use it again and again. Practice it first with a thick rope like a clothesline.

Motor Bug Roach Coach

It's a brown terror on wheels. The Roach Coach dashes across your floor like a real — and enormous — roach. Your parents will love it.

To power the Roach Coach, use a mini-size rev car or pull-back car. A Matchbox-type push car will work fine, too, or use wheels from a construction set like Lego.

You Need:

1 toy car OR set of wheels from a construction set
1 sheet of brown construction paper (9″ × 12″)
1 sheet of tracing paper OR typing paper
black marker
cellophane tape
Tools: ruler, pencil, scissors

1. Pick a toy car and measure it. It should be no longer than 3″ and no wider than 1¼″. Many little cars will fit perfectly.

2. Fold a sheet of brown construction paper so the long sides meet.

3. Page 8 shows you an easy way to copy the full-size pattern on the facing page onto your folded construction paper. Be sure that the straight centerline of the pattern lies along the fold of the paper.

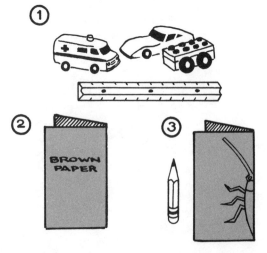

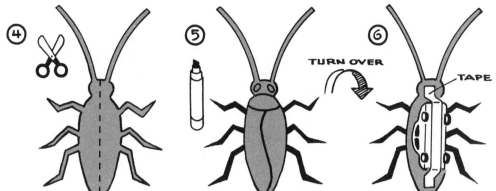

4. Cut through both sides of the paper at once along the outline. Be careful around the legs and the long antennae.

5. Decorate the roach. Color the legs black and outline the wings, head, and eyes in black.

6. Tape your car to the bottom of the paper roach.

7. Shape the paper roach around the car by bending the sides down till the legs almost touch the floor. Bend the long antennae back over the body the way roaches usually carry them. Your Roach Coach is ready to roll.

More Motor Bugs

All your little cars can be transformed into Motor Bugs. Just follow the directions for the Roach Coach but use different bugs. Make a beetle or a weevil, a borer or a caterpillar, or make up your own wonderful imaginary Motor Bug. Copy your bug from a book about insects or copy him out of your dreams. You could even catch a real bug and copy him.

PUT CENTERLINE ON FOLD

FULL-SIZE PATTERN

A Bat in Your Hat

Wearing a hat, you walk into a room where your friends are. Your hands are on your hat and you have a worried look on your face. "This is really weird," you say. "Something is fluttering around inside my hat. Wow! I never felt anything *this* strange!"

Then you lift up your hat and a bat flies out and hovers right over your head.

The black thread that the bat hangs from is almost invisible, so it looks just like it's suspended in air.

You Need:
    1 piece of black construction paper
    1 piece of tracing paper OR typing paper
    1 bobby pin
    cellophane tape
    glue stick OR white glue
    1 hat
    Tools: pencil, scissors, ruler, black pen,
             needle, black sewing thread

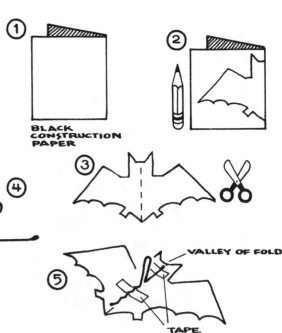

1. Fold a piece of black construction paper in half.

2. Copy the pattern on the facing page onto your construction paper. (Page 8 shows you an easy way to do this.) Make sure the straight centerline of the pattern lies along the fold of the black paper.

3. Cut through both sides of the paper at once along the outline and then open up your bat.

4. Bend a bobby pin into this shape:

5. Tape the bobby pin in the valley fold of the bat shape, using small pieces of tape.

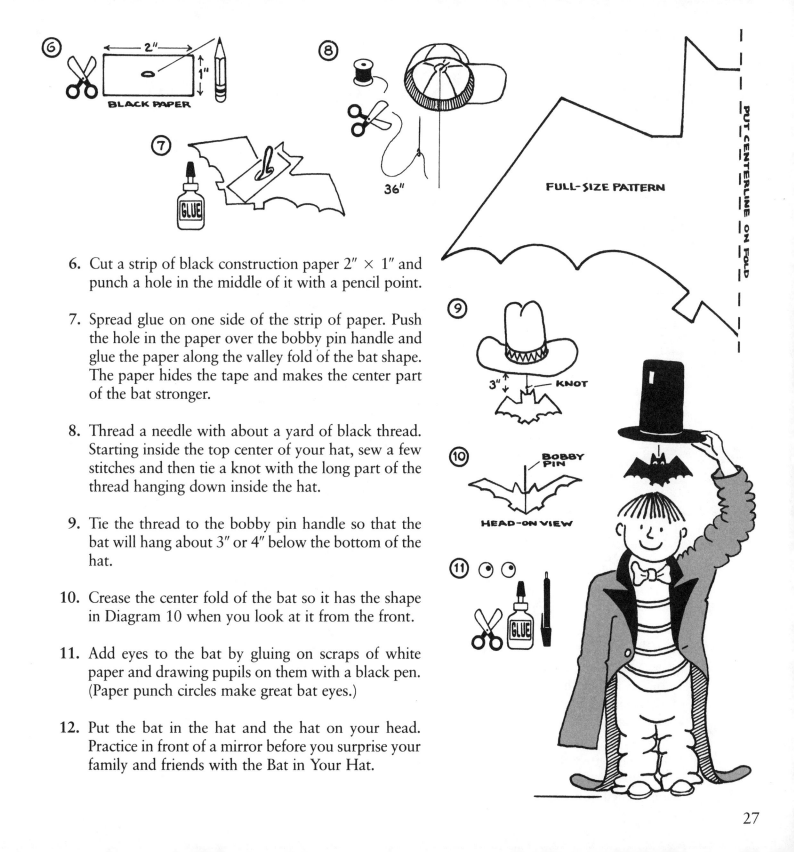

⑥ **BLACK PAPER** — 2" × 1"

⑧ 36"

FULL-SIZE PATTERN

PUT CENTERLINE ON FOLD

⑨ 3" ↕ KNOT

⑩ **BOBBY PIN** / **HEAD-ON VIEW**

⑪

6. Cut a strip of black construction paper 2″ × 1″ and punch a hole in the middle of it with a pencil point.

7. Spread glue on one side of the strip of paper. Push the hole in the paper over the bobby pin handle and glue the paper along the valley fold of the bat shape. The paper hides the tape and makes the center part of the bat stronger.

8. Thread a needle with about a yard of black thread. Starting inside the top center of your hat, sew a few stitches and then tie a knot with the long part of the thread hanging down inside the hat.

9. Tie the thread to the bobby pin handle so that the bat will hang about 3″ or 4″ below the bottom of the hat.

10. Crease the center fold of the bat so it has the shape in Diagram 10 when you look at it from the front.

11. Add eyes to the bat by gluing on scraps of white paper and drawing pupils on them with a black pen. (Paper punch circles make great bat eyes.)

12. Put the bat in the hat and the hat on your head. Practice in front of a mirror before you surprise your family and friends with the Bat in Your Hat.

27

Circling Butterflies

Six butterflies chase each other in circles as this pinwheel spins. Wave it through the air or run with it to make it swirl. It's easy to make if you're good with a pair of scissors.

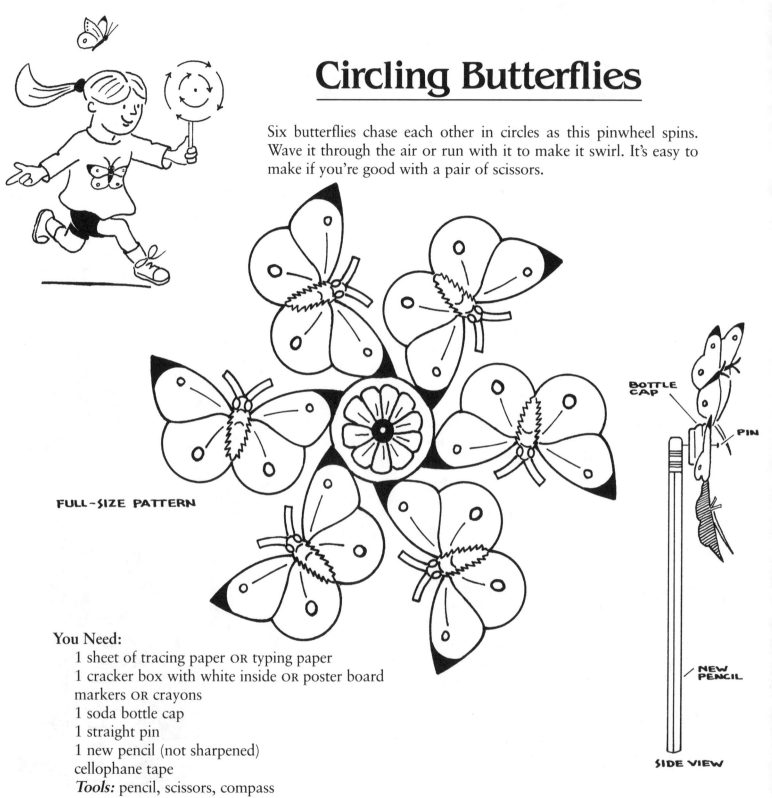

FULL-SIZE PATTERN

BOTTLE CAP

PIN

NEW PENCIL

SIDE VIEW

You Need:
1 sheet of tracing paper OR typing paper
1 cracker box with white inside OR poster board
markers OR crayons
1 soda bottle cap
1 straight pin
1 new pencil (not sharpened)
cellophane tape
Tools: pencil, scissors, compass

28

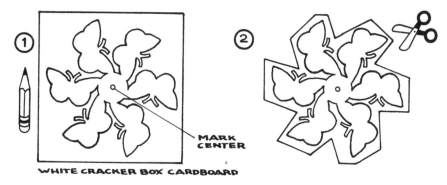

WHITE CRACKER BOX CARDBOARD

MARK CENTER

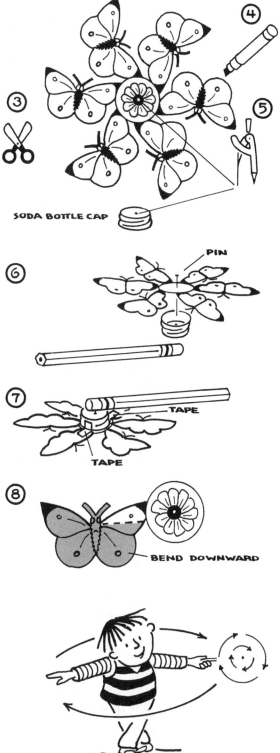

SODA BOTTLE CAP

PIN

TAPE

TAPE

BEND DOWNWARD

1. Page 8 shows you an easy way to copy the outline of the full-size pattern on the facing page onto white cracker box cardboard or poster board. Make sure to mark the center point.

2. Rough-cut the whole design from the cardboard.

3. Cut carefully around the butterflies.

4. Decorate the butterflies with markers or crayons.

5. With a compass point, make a small center hole in the pinwheel and another in the soda bottle cap.

6. Put a straight pin through the hole in the pinwheel, then through the hole in the bottle cap, from the inside. Push the pinpoint into the eraser of a new pencil. Be sure to use a brand-new pencil with no point.

7. Use two small pieces of tape to join the bottle cap to the back of the pinwheel.

8. IMPORTANT: On each butterfly, imagine a dotted line like the one in the diagram (Step 8). Bend — don't fold — the shaded part of each butterfly downward from the line to give the pinwheel the shape that makes it spin.

29

Giant Attack Bug

Buzz your family and friends with the biggest mosquito on the block. It's easy to operate: just say "ZZZZZZZZZ" and chase someone you love with the Giant Attack Bug. It strikes fear into the hearts of all who see it.

You Need:
1 white 5″ × 8″ index card
1 sheet of tracing paper OR typing paper
colored markers
Tools: pencil, scissors, black pen

Mosquito Buzzing

A real mosquito makes her happy, friendly buzz by beating her little wings 300 to 500 times each second. That's a lot of wing beating.

Try flapping your arms 500 times in a second. No way! Now get someone with a stopwatch to time you and see if you can flap your arms even 5 times in a second. Hold your arms out straight. Flap higher than your head and lower than your waist. Shorter flaps don't count.

If you can flap the full 5 times a second you are a true Mosquito Kid. If you make it to 10, your arms may start to buzz. At 15 times a second you will probably take off. But remember: No matter how good you get at flapping, the real mosquito has you beat at *500* times a second.

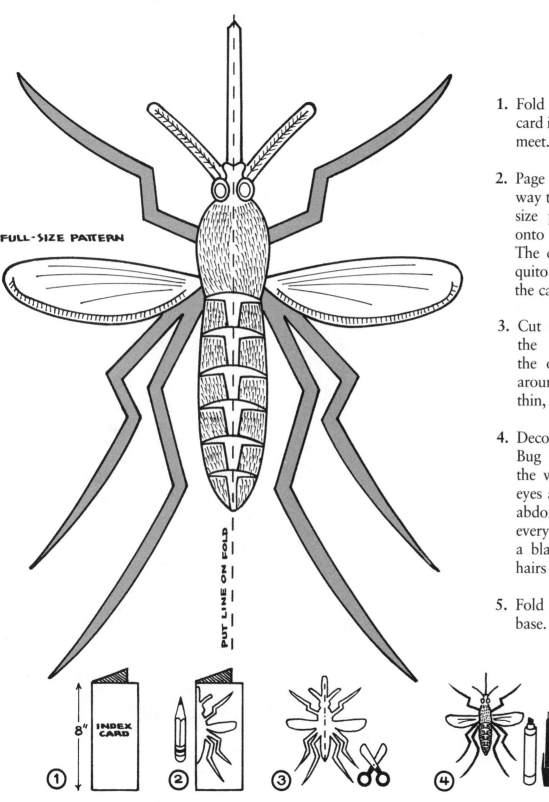

FULL-SIZE PATTERN

PUT LINE ON FOLD

8" INDEX CARD

① ② ③ ④ ⑤ FOLD WINGS UP

1. Fold a 5″ × 8″ white index card in half so the long sides meet.

2. Page 8 shows you an easy way to copy half of the full-size pattern on this page onto the folded index card. The centerline of the mosquito goes along the fold of the card.

3. Cut through both sides of the card at once along the outline. Snip carefully around the long legs and the thin, stinging proboscis.

4. Decorate the Giant Attack Bug with markers. Make the wings light yellow, the eyes and the pattern on the abdomen deep yellow, and everything else brown. Use a black pen to draw little hairs all over the body.

5. Fold the wings up at their base.

31

Batburgers

All the little ghouls drool when Daddy Dracula ties on his apron and fires up the grill to barbecue the Batburgers.

Batburgers are served folded in their own wings and should be eaten dripping with catsup blood.

Along with Batburgers, Dracula and his kids always eat fat French fries called Frankenstein Fingers. There are five fries in a serving of Frankenstein Fingers — a handful, that is.

You Need:
   hamburger meat
   sliced bread
   olives
   catsup

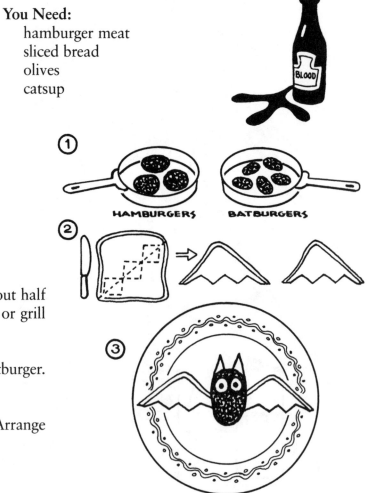

1. Make Batburgers in an oblong shape and about half the size of your usual hamburgers. Fry, broil, or grill them.

2. One slice of bread makes both wings for a Batburger. Toast the bread before cutting it.

3. Make the ears from leftover scraps of bread. Arrange the bat on a plate and add olive-slice eyes.

4. For a Cheese Batburger, melt a slice of cheese on the burger. For a Bacon Batburger, add two strips of bacon. For a Vampire Batburger, take your first bite from the Batburger's neck.

Drink Like a Vampire Bat

A vampire bat cuts his victims with razor-sharp teeth. Then he curls his tongue into the shape of a tube, puts it into the wound, and slurps out the blood just as if he were using a soda straw.

It's too bad that kids don't have razor-sharp teeth. But you *do* have a batlike tongue. Try curling it lengthwise into a vampire bat straw. It's easy to do for a lot of us. The edges curl right up and meet. Now drink from a small glass of fruit punch, cranberry juice, or V-8 with your tongue.

Your mom and dad will probably hate this trick because it's a little disgusting. Be sure to tell them it's okay since it's *educational* — nature study.

Vampire bats all live in Mexico and South America, but even if you go there, they won't attack you, since their victims are mostly cattle. A vampire bat is tiny; he weighs only an ounce — about as much as three Oreo cookies — but he can drink as much as half an ounce of fresh blood, or half his own weight. If you drank half of your own weight in soda, how many two-liter bottles would you have to guzzle? **Hint:** A two-liter bottle weighs about four pounds.

Filled with so much extra weight, the vampire bat can't fly away as soon as he finishes drinking blood. Is he stuck there on the cow? What happens if the cow rolls over or flicks her big tail at the overstuffed bat? No problem. Vampire bats have extra-strong, heavy-duty rear legs to hop away on. That's right, a hopping bat. See how far *you* can hop after drinking all those two-liter bottles of soda.

High-Climb Butterfly

Pull the strings apart and the butterfly takes off, soaring straight up. Relax the strings and the butterfly slips back down, ready for another climb.

You Need:
    1 piece of construction paper
    1 piece of tracing paper OR typing paper
    1 plastic soda straw
    cellophane tape
    very light string OR sewing thread
    Tools: pencil, scissors, black pen, ruler

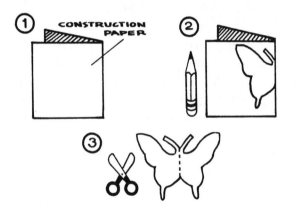

1. Fold a piece of colored construction paper in half.

2. Copy the pattern on the facing page onto the construction paper. (Page 8 shows you an easy way to do this.) Make sure the straight centerline of the design lies along the fold of the paper.

3. Cut through both sides of the paper at once along the outline. Be careful cutting around the antennae and the swallowtails.

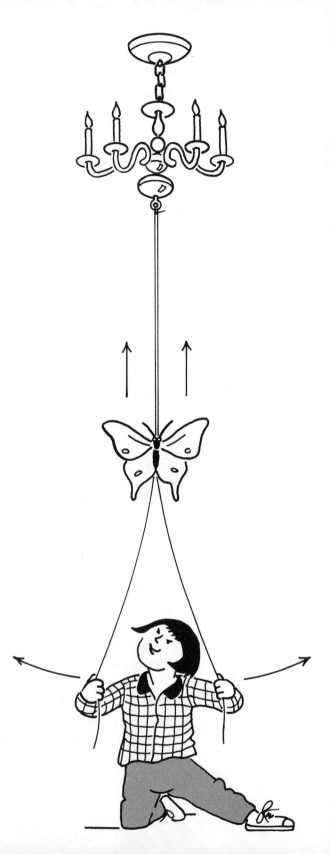

4. Decorate one side of the butterfly with a black pen. For fancier decorations, cut and glue on pieces of colored paper, or use glue and glitter to make the wings sparkle.

5. Cut a piece of soda straw 1½″ long. Wrap one end of it tightly with two or three turns of tape to make it stronger.

6. Tape the straw to the back of the butterfly. The strong end goes at the bottom.

7. Get a grown-up to help you attach your light string or thread to a high place. The string should be at least twice as long as the height you will reach. The middle of the string is attached, so you have two long ends hanging down.

8. Thread the string ends through the straw. They will go through easily if you push them into the top and then suck lightly on the other end of the straw.

9. Pull the strings apart and up goes the butterfly.

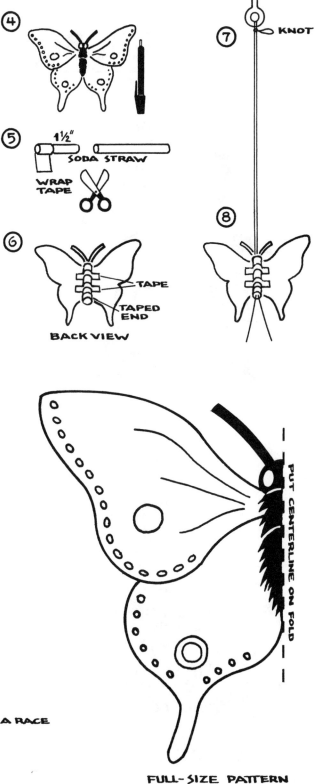

④

⑤ 1½″ SODA STRAW
WRAP TAPE

⑥ TAPE
TAPED END
BACK VIEW

⑦ KNOT

⑧

MAKE TWO FOR A RACE

PUT CENTERLINE ON FOLD

FULL-SIZE PATTERN

Stink Bugs and Perfume Bugs

The stink bug is the skunk of the insect world. When you pick up a real stink bug, he squirts a sickly sweet stink juice on your hand, and it doesn't wash off.

You can make two kinds of *play* stink bugs.

One is a pretty Perfume Bug that smells just great. Give Perfume Bugs to friends as presents and keep them in your purse or drawer for a special sniff.

The other kind is a real *stinker*. Your friends will be disgusted when they find these Stink Bugs lurking where you've hidden them.

Follow the instructions to make a realistic-looking Stink Bug, or invent your own original, imaginary Perfume Bug or Stink Bug. Make it look beautiful for perfume, or evil and smelly.

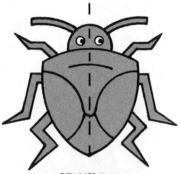

STINK BUG
FULL-SIZE PATTERN
PUT CENTERLINE ON FOLD

You Need:
> 1 sheet of green construction paper
> 1 sheet of tracing paper OR typing paper
> 1 clean, dry new sponge
> white glue
> perfume OR something wet and stinky
> *Tools:* pencil, scissors, black pen, ruler

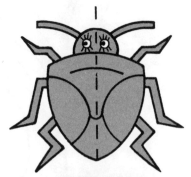

PERFUME BUG
FULL-SIZE PATTERN
PUT CENTERLINE ON FOLD

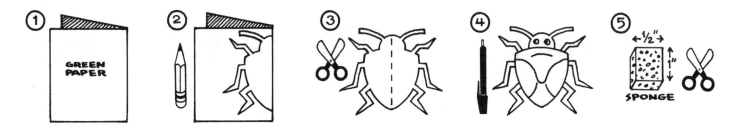

1. Fold a piece of green construction paper in half.

2. Page 8 shows you an easy way to copy half of the full-size pattern on the facing page onto your paper. Be sure the centerline of the pattern lies along the fold of the paper.

3. Cut through both sides of the paper at once along the outline. Snip carefully around the tiny legs and antennae. Open up your paper bug.

4. Decorate the bug with a black pen. Leave his legs and antennae green, since real stink bugs are green all over.

5. Cut a rectangle of clean, dry new sponge about ½″ × 1″.

6. Glue the little sponge to the bottom of the bug.

7. When the glue is dry, soak the sponge with some wonderful smell. The choice is yours. Will it be a pretty perfume, or something vile, foul, and gross?

Magnetic Bat

Flying this tiny bat will give you a nice spooky feeling.

You Need:
    1 sheet of tracing paper OR typing paper
    1 sheet of black tissue paper
    black sewing thread
    1 paper clip
    cellophane tape
    1 magnet
    Tools: pencil, scissors, ruler

FULL-SIZE PATTERN

1. Transfer the full-size pattern onto the black tissue paper. (Page 8 shows you an easy way to do this.)

2. Cut out the little tissue paper bat.

3. Cut a piece of sewing thread about 4′ long.

4. Tape one end of the thread to a hard floor. Tie the other end to a paper clip and attach the paper clip to the bat.

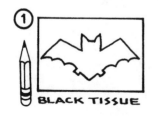

BLACK TISSUE

④
PAPER CLIP
KNOT
TAPE
4′

5. Find the strongest magnet in your house. Catch the paper clip and bat with the magnet and pull up till the thread is tight. Now gently pull the magnet up away from the bat so it is just above it but not touching. How far away can you move the magnet without dropping the bat out of its magnetic sky? Try moving the magnet slowly to one side. If you're careful, you can get the bat to follow and "fly" at a steep angle to the floor. If this bat doesn't fly for you, you need a stronger magnet.

THREE BLIND BATS

Are Bats Really Blind?

Have you ever heard someone shout at a baseball umpire, "You're as blind as a bat!"? Well, everyone knows that umpires are blind, but are bats really blind? Yes and no.

Our little North American bats are almost blind in the eyes, but they *see* perfectly — with their ears. While people live in a bright daytime world of sights where eyes are all-important, bats live in a dark nighttime world of sounds, and they see by listening with their big, super-keen ears.

As a bat flies through the darkness, he makes high-pitched sounds — so high that people can't hear them. The sounds bounce, or echo, off all nearby objects. The returning echoes give the bat a perfect picture of the world around him. He can hear exactly where walls and trees are and can fly around them. Even more important, his echo-location system can find tiny moving things, like the insects he eats by the thousands every night. He easily spots flying mosquitoes and moths and catches them in midair.

With such great hearing, an insect-eating bat doesn't really need good eyes. Hold a piece of tracing paper or thin typing paper in front of your eyes and you'll get an idea of what he can see with his eyes — not much. He can see the difference between big areas of light and dark but no details. You can blindfold a bat and set him loose and he will still fly perfectly, seeing with his ears.

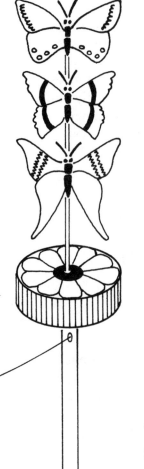

Butterfly Twirler

The butterflies spin so fast you can see right through them — like ghost butterflies.

Pull the thread to set the butterflies spinning. Relax your pull and they keep spinning. Pull again and they spin in the opposite direction. Relax. Pull. Relax. Pull. Keep it up. Find a rhythm and the butterflies keep whirling.

You Need:
colored paper
1 bamboo skewer (from a supermarket)
1 plastic soda straw
sewing thread (heavy-duty is best)
1 plastic milk bottle cap
cellophane tape
sandpaper
Tools: pencil, ruler, scissors, compass, black pen

FULL SIZE

FULL SIZE

1. Fold three small pieces of colored paper in half.

2. With a pencil draw three half butterfly shapes with antennae on the colored paper. The centerline of each butterfly should lie along the fold of the paper. Make the shapes plain or fancy, as you like, but make them no more than ¾″ from centerline to wing tip. The butterflies along the bottoms of these pages are the right size. If you would like to copy them, turn to page 8 for an easy copying method.

3. Cut through both sides of the paper at once along the outlines. Snip carefully around the antennae. Open out your three butterfly shapes.

4. With a compass, draw on colored paper a circle about the size of your plastic milk bottle cap. Cut it out. This will be the flower.

5. Draw details on the butterflies and flower with a black pen. Copy the designs on the butterflies from these pages or use your imagination.

6. Break off the point of a bamboo skewer and sand its ends smooth. You can use a ⅛″ dowel instead of a skewer — make it 11½″ long and sand its ends smooth.

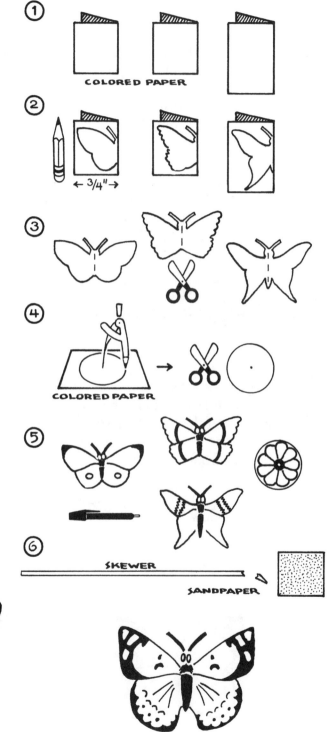

7. With the point of a compass, punch a hole in the center of the plastic milk bottle cap. Enlarge the hole with the compass until you can just push the dowel or skewer through it.

8. Push the milk bottle cap onto the stick so the top of it is about 5" from one end. It should fit tightly around the stick.

9. Push the stick through the center hole of the paper flower. The flower will rest on top of the milk bottle cap.

10. Tape the butterflies to the stick with small pieces of tape.

11. With the point of your compass, punch a hole in the side of a plastic soda straw 1" from the end of the straw.

12. Cut a piece of sewing thread 16" long. Thread one end of it into the hole you made in Step 11 and then out the end of the straw nearer the hole. Sucking on the end of the straw will help pull the thread through.

13. Tie the end of the thread *tightly* around the stick 1" below the bottom of the bottle cap.

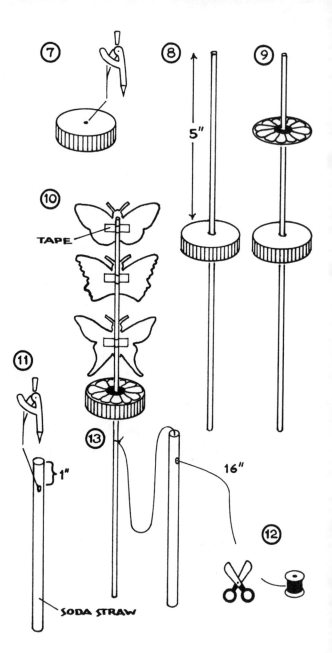

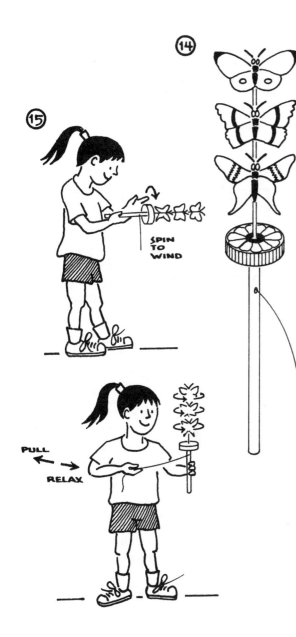

14. Put the long end of the stick into the soda straw and pull the free end of the thread all the way out of the hole in the straw. The Butterfly Twirler is ready to go.

15. Hold the soda straw handle in one hand. With your other hand, spin the bottle cap flywheel to wrap most of the thread around the stick inside the soda straw handle. Now pull briskly on the thread *before you pull out the whole way,* relax your pull, and the flywheel will keep spinning until the thread is wound onto the stick again. Pull again. Relax. Pull. Relax. Keep it up and find the rhythm.

Tips

- The thread may cut the side of the soda straw as it travels back and forth. If it does, make the hole larger with the point of a pencil so the thread can move freely.
- If the knot you tied in Step 13 isn't tight enough, the thread may slip and make the Butterfly Twirler slow down or stop. Tie it again more tightly. If that doesn't do the trick, wrap the thread several times around the stick, tie a tight knot, and coat it with white glue. Wait for it to dry completely before using the toy again.

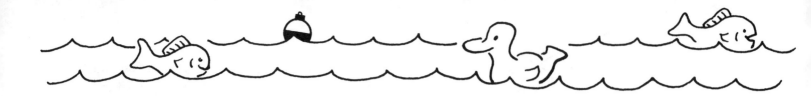

Wind-up Water Bug

The biggest and liveliest bug in your bathtub. A rubber band and paddle wheel drive this floating Styrofoam bug quickly through the water. Make two for a race.

The Styrofoam version is a little bigger than the real thing, but a giant water bug is a huge critter. He can be almost three inches long — so big that he eats tadpoles and even little frogs. He is the king of the pond and a terrible bully. If you find a real giant water bug, don't pick him up. His bite is *very* mean and includes a mild dose of poison.

Some people call the giant water bug the electric light bug because at night he flies up out of his pond and heads straight for the nearest light bulb.

You Need:
    1 sheet of tracing paper
      OR typing paper
    1 Styrofoam meat tray
    1 rubber band
    Tools: pencil, scissors, black
      ballpoint pen

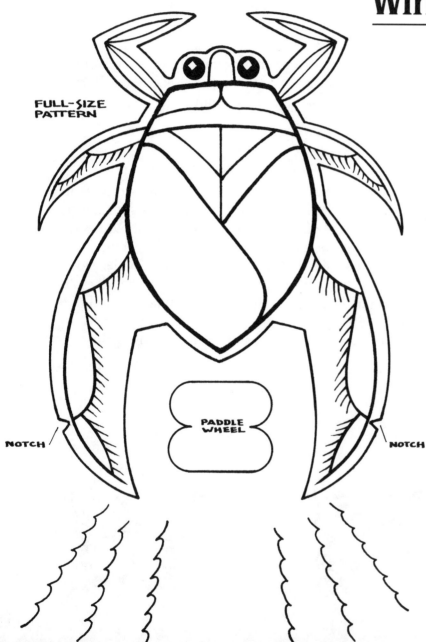

FULL-SIZE PATTERN

PADDLE WHEEL

NOTCH

NOTCH

1. On tracing paper or typing paper trace the outline of the Water Bug on the facing page. Also trace the paddle wheel.

2. Put your copy on a Styrofoam meat tray. Pressing hard with a dull pencil, follow the outlines to transfer the patterns to the Styrofoam.

3. With scissors, rough-cut around the Water Bug and paddle wheel. Then carefully cut around the legs. Make sure to cut small notches on the sides of the rear legs for the rubber band.

4. Use a black ballpoint pen to decorate the Water Bug. Copy the lines on the full-size pattern to make it look like a real water bug, or make up a design of your own.

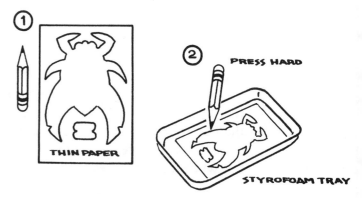

① THIN PAPER

② PRESS HARD STYROFOAM TRAY

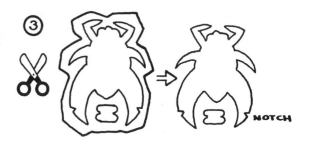

③ NOTCH

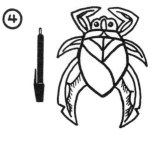

④

5. Pick out a lightweight rubber band that fits snugly around the notches on the rear legs without stretching much.

6. Fill the tub.

7. Slip the paddle wheel inside the loop formed by the rubber band. Turn the paddle wheel many times so that the rubber band is wound tightly around it. Set the bug in the water and let 'er rip. Like any rubber band toy, the Water Bug runs out of energy quickly, but while it's alive it really moves.

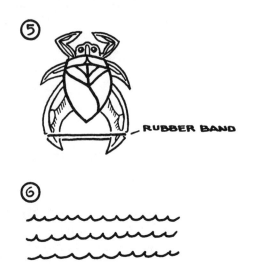

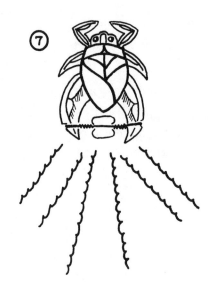

Whirly Bat

Drop the Whirly Bat from a high place or toss it hard and toss it high. This easy-to-make toy spins as it travels. Its twirling action looks a lot like the fluttering flight of a bat.

You Need:
    1 sheet of tracing paper OR typing paper
    1 sheet of black construction paper
    1 pen or marker cap (see Step 3)
    cellophane tape
    Tools: pencil, scissors

1. Copy the full-size bat pattern on this page onto black construction paper. (Page 8 shows you an easy way to do this.)

① BLACK CONSTRUCTION PAPER

②

FULL-SIZE PATTERN

2. Cut out the bat.

3. Find a pen or marker cap with a pocket clip that sticks out past the end of the cap. (If you can't find a cap like this, almost any pen or marker cap can be used, but it won't work quite as well.) Black is the best color for the pen or marker cap.

4. Tape the bat to the pocket clip of the pen cap. If you use a cap without a pocket clip, tape the bat directly to the pen cap, with the bat's head and shoulders extending beyond the open end of the cap.

5. The tops of the wings are shaded in Diagram 5. Bend (don't fold) these wing tops down in opposite directions (toward the opposite sides of the bat) to create the propeller shape that makes the toy twirl.

6. Check to make sure that the side view of the finished Whirly Bat looks like the side view shown in Diagram 6.

7. Throw the toy with the pen cap out in front and watch it spin. Outdoors, toss it as high as you can underhanded. It spins on the way up and on the way down.

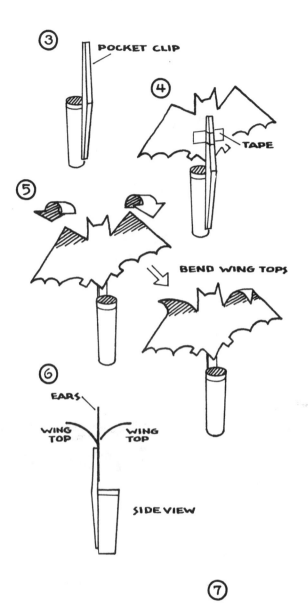

49

PUSH WITH
RIGHT HAND

IT SPINS

IT CLIMBS

Buttercopter

A high-climbing hand-launched helicopter toy. As the two butterflies of the rotor chase each other in circles, they drive the copter up into the sky.

The Buttercopter flies well indoors or out, but indoors you'll want to be in a room with a pretty high ceiling.

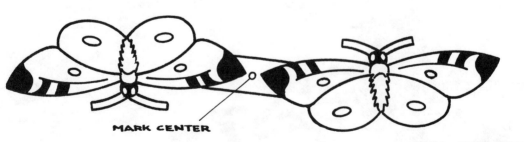

MARK CENTER

FULL-SIZE PATTERN

You Need:
- 1 cracker box with white inside
   OR poster board
- 1 sheet of tracing paper OR typing paper
- 1 bamboo skewer (from a supermarket)
- sandpaper
- white glue OR hot-melt glue
- markers OR crayons
- *Tools:* scissors, compass, pencil, ruler

1. Page 8 shows you an easy way to copy the outline of the full-size pattern on the facing page onto your cracker box cardboard or poster board.

2. With a compass point, punch a hole at the center. Work the tool around in the hole to make it just big enough for your bamboo skewer to fit snugly in it.

3. Cut out the butterflies, taking special care around the antennae.

4. Color the butterflies with markers or crayons.

5. Break a 6½″ piece from the bamboo skewer. Rub the ends smooth with sandpaper.

6. Push one end of the stick through the center hole of the rotor so the rotor is about ⅛″ from the end of the stick. Glue both above and below where the stick and the rotor meet. White glue will take at least an hour to dry. If you have hot-melt glue, use it with help from a grown-up and your Buttercopter will be ready to fly in minutes. Make sure the stick and the rotor are glued together at right angles.

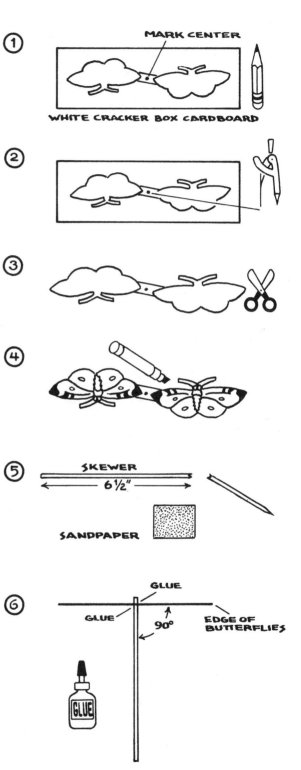

① MARK CENTER

WHITE CRACKER BOX CARDBOARD

②

③

④

⑤ SKEWER
← 6½″ →

SANDPAPER

⑥ GLUE
GLUE
90°
EDGE OF BUTTERFLIES
GLUE

7. When the glue is fully dry, take each butterfly between the thumb and first finger of one hand. Now twist the rear edge of each butterfly downward to create the propeller shape that gives the Buttercopter lift. Try to give an even amount of twist on each side of the rotor. Now it's ready to go.

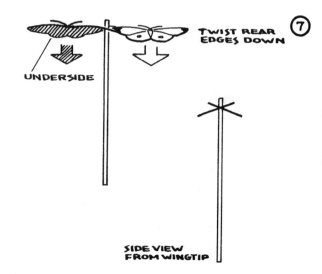

UNDERSIDE

TWIST REAR EDGES DOWN

⑦

SIDE VIEW FROM WINGTIP

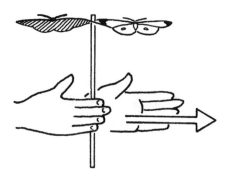

Flying Tips

- Hold the stick firmly between the fingers of your right hand and the heel of your left hand.
- Push your right hand forward rapidly, rolling the stick along the palm and fingers of your left hand. At the end of your push, pull your hands apart and the spinning Buttercopter will take off.
- A little practice makes perfect.
- If the Buttercopter flies *down,* the rotor is on upside down. Just reverse hands: Start with the stick between the fingers of your left hand and the heel of your right hand. Now it will go *up.*

Bug Chopper

A tiny helicopter that spins swiftly up to the ceiling. Launch this little chopper the way you twirl a spinning top — only upside down.

Two ladybugs make up the rotor, so as you set the toy spinning you can say, "Ladybug, ladybug, fly away home!"

You Need:

1 sheet of tracing paper OR typing paper
1 white 3″ × 5″ index card
1 toothpick (round OR flat)
white glue OR hot-melt glue
markers OR crayons
Tools: pencil, compass, scissors

FULL-SIZE PATTERN

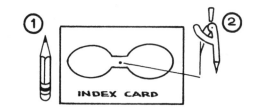

INDEX CARD

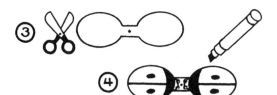

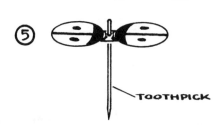

TOOTHPICK

1. Copy the full-size pattern on this page onto a white index card; see page 8 for an easy way to do this.

2. With a compass point, punch a small center hole.

3. Cut out the ladybugs.

4. Color them red with black spots. Some ladybugs have two spots; some have nine.

5. Put one end of the toothpick (the thick end if you use a flat toothpick) through the center hole so it sticks out about ¼″ above the rotor.

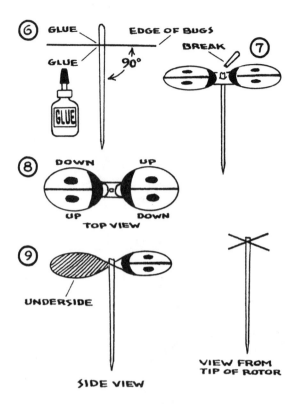

GLUE   EDGE OF BUGS

GLUE   90°

BREAK

DOWN   UP

UP   DOWN
TOP VIEW

UNDERSIDE

SIDE VIEW

VIEW FROM
TIP OF ROTOR

6. Put glue both above and below where the toothpick and the rotor meet. White glue here will take at least an hour to dry. If you have hot-melt glue, use it with help from a grown-up and your Bug Chopper will be ready to fly in minutes. Be sure the parts are glued together at right angles.

7. When the glue is fully dry, break off the top end of the toothpick close to the rotor.

8. Hold one ladybug between the thumb and first finger of each hand. Twist into a propeller shape. Diagram 8 shows the directions to twist in.

9. See Diagram 9 for a side view of the Bug Chopper ready to fly.

Flying Tips

- The Bug Chopper works like a spinning top — only upside down.
- Hold the lower end of the toothpick between your thumb and first finger.
- **Right-handers:** Start with the toothpick on the side of your first finger near the other fingers. Roll it toward the outside of the finger.
- **Lefties:** Start with the toothpick on the outside of your first finger and roll it toward the other fingers.
- The bugs must spin with their up-bent edges leading. If the down-bent edges lead, the chopper will fly downward.
- To improve the Bug Chopper's performance, from time to time re-twist the propeller the way you did in Step 8. Experiment with different amounts of twist to get a perfect spin.

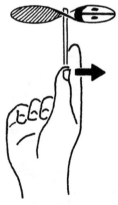

RIGHT HAND

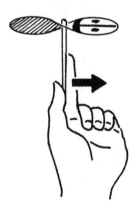

LEFT HAND

Bat Glider

The Bat Glider is a fantastic flier. It slices through the air, does high loops, spirals slowly down and around, catches on passing breezes, and goes and goes.

Throw this little bat as hard as you can. It loves being really whipped into the air. The harder your throw, the higher it climbs and the farther it glides. Indoors, throw it gently or it will climb and hit the ceiling before it has a chance to travel across the room.

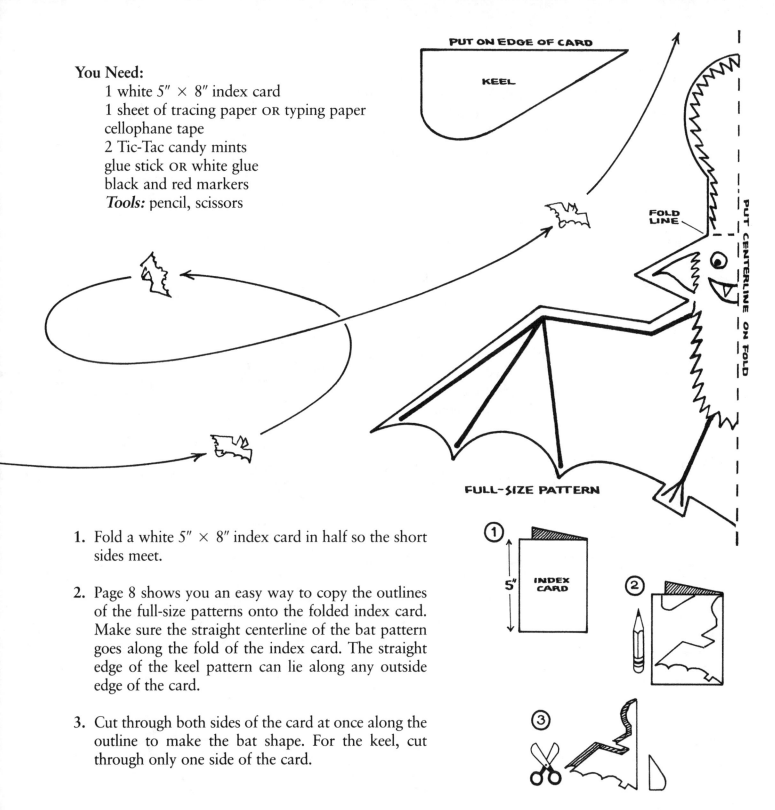

You Need:
> 1 white 5″ × 8″ index card
> 1 sheet of tracing paper OR typing paper
> cellophane tape
> 2 Tic-Tac candy mints
> glue stick OR white glue
> black and red markers
> *Tools:* pencil, scissors

PUT ON EDGE OF CARD

KEEL

FOLD LINE

PUT CENTERLINE ON FOLD

FULL-SIZE PATTERN

1. Fold a white 5″ × 8″ index card in half so the short sides meet.

2. Page 8 shows you an easy way to copy the outlines of the full-size patterns onto the folded index card. Make sure the straight centerline of the bat pattern goes along the fold of the index card. The straight edge of the keel pattern can lie along any outside edge of the card.

3. Cut through both sides of the card at once along the outline to make the bat shape. For the keel, cut through only one side of the card.

① 5″ INDEX CARD

②

③

57

4. Copy the design from the full-size pattern onto the side with the hill of the fold. Make the mouth and ears red and the rest of the lines black. Turn the bat over. On the side with the valley of the fold, use a black marker to draw the bones in the wings, and the legs and feet.

5. Fold the bat shape and lay it on a table. Lay the keel in place next to it with a tiny gap (¹⁄₁₆″) between them. Tape the keel and the bat together.

6. Turn the bat over and tape the other side. Snip off corners of tape that stick out past the edges of the bat and the keel.

7. Open the wings and lay the bat on a table with the valley-fold side up and the keel folded to one side under it. Fold up the U-shaped section, which will form the bat's body, on the line between the two ears.

8. Two Tic-Tac candy mints give the weight that pulls the glider forward through the air. Lay two Tic-Tacs in the corner made by the U-shaped body section and the head, and tape them in place.

9. Spread glue on the side of the body with the Tic-Tacs. Bend it down and glue it in place. A glue stick is quick; white glue here takes half an hour to dry.

10. Fold up the ears.

11. Bend the points along the rear edges of the wings up slightly. If they are bent down, the glider will nose-dive.

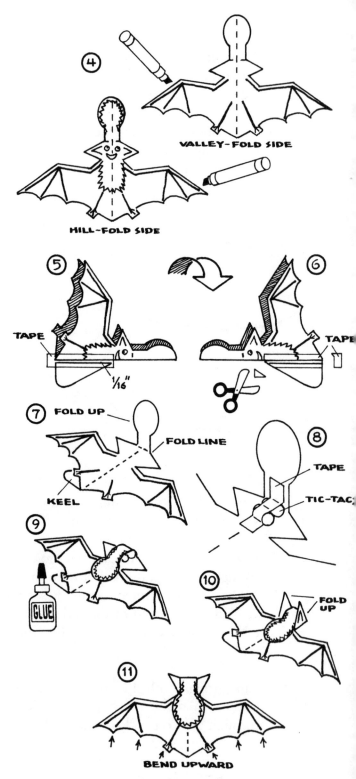

58

Flying Tips

- Before launching, look at the glider head-on from the front. The wings should be held up in a wide V with the keel straight down.
- To launch the glider, hold the keel between your thumb and middle finger with your first finger along its back edge. Then throw it as you would throw any glider.
- Outdoors, throw the glider upward as hard as you can. Throw it either into the face of an oncoming breeze or in the same direction the breeze is going. Don't throw it *across* the breeze. The glider will perform well on a calm day, but light gusty winds will really make it travel. Fall days around Halloween are ideal for flying this bat.
- If the glider curves to one side over and over again instead of flying straight, the keel is probably bent. Straighten and smooth it with your fingers. If that doesn't correct the curving, try shifting the nose weight a little bit away from the side the glider curves toward.

If People Had Wings Like Bats'

People and bats are a lot alike. We are both mammals, for instance, so we both feed our babies with milk.

If people had wings like bats', our babies would look like the one in the picture. A bat's wing is its arm and hand with the fingers grown *very* long and a thin skin, or membrane, stretched between the fingers. Another membrane stretches between the hand and the side and leg of the bat — or the baby, in this case. In most bats there is also a membrane stretched between the legs. Some bats have a tail in the middle of this membrane, but of course babies don't have tails. Bats can use their wings like hands to grab insects in midair and scoop them into their mouths. They even have a useful hooklike thumb at the top of the wing where you see the winged baby's thumb.

Don't you wish you had been such a cute baby?

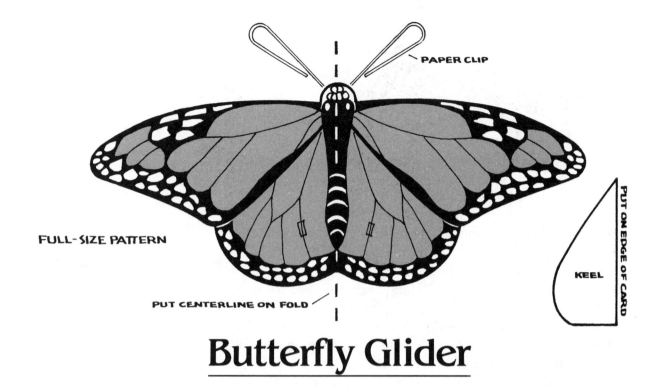

FULL-SIZE PATTERN

PAPER CLIP

PUT CENTERLINE ON FOLD

KEEL

PUT ON EDGE OF CARD

Butterfly Glider

This glider is as graceful in flight as the monarch butterfly it imitates. Its shape is a copy of the wings of the monarch, and this gives it some of the monarch's powerful flying ability. A real monarch flies so well that he can wing it from New York to Mexico. Throw the Butterfly Glider as high as you can. It will climb, trace a perfect loop, level out, and head for Mexico.

The glider's antennae are made from paper clips bent in a special shape and taped to the bottom of the wings. Their weight pulls the glider forward through the air. A real butterfly's thin antennae of course have almost no weight at all. Many people think the butterfly uses them as "feelers," which is not true. In fact, the butterfly *smells* with his antennae.

You Need:
    1 white 4″ × 6″ index card
    1 sheet of tracing paper OR typing paper
    cellophane tape
    3 regular-size paper clips (see Step 7)
    markers OR crayons
    Tools: pencil, scissors

60

1. Fold a 4″ × 6″ white index card in half so the short sides meet.

2. Page 8 shows you an easy way to copy the outline of half of the full-size pattern on the facing page onto the folded index card. Make sure the centerline of the pattern goes along the fold of the index card. The straight edge of the keel pattern can lie along any outside edge of the card.

3. Cut through both sides of the index card at the same time along the outline to make the butterfly shape. For the keel shape, cut through only one side of the card.

4. Leave the butterfly shape folded and lay it on a tabletop. Lay the keel in place next to it with a tiny gap (1/16″) between them. Now tape the butterfly and the keel together with a single strip of tape.

5. Turn over and tape the other side. Snip off corners of tape that stick out past the edges of the butterfly and the keel.

6. Open the wings and lay the butterfly on a table with the keel folded to one side under it. Decorate the up side (top) of the Butterfly Glider with markers or crayons. Make up any pattern or combination of colors you like, or make it look like a real butterfly. For a very realistic glider, you can copy the monarch butterfly markings shown on the full-size pattern. The markings are black; color all larger spots on the wings orange and leave the small spots on the borders of the wings white.

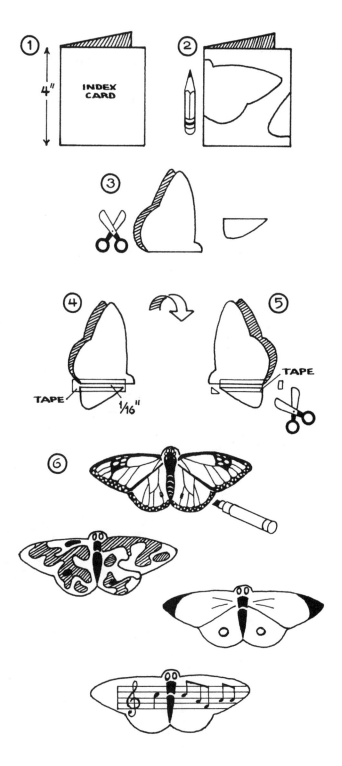

7. The Butterfly Glider's antennae are made from paper clips. They give the glider the weight that pulls it forward, so it is important to use exactly the right size of paper clips to get the right amount of weight. Use regular-size paper clips from a variety store, exactly the size shown. Other sizes won't work as well.

8. Bend three paper clips open into the shape shown. Hold them against the illustration to be sure you get the shape right, and hold them against each other to be sure they are all the same.

9. Fold the glider and tape a paper clip to it.

10. Turn the folded butterfly over and tape another paper clip to the other side. Line this one up exactly with the first one.

11. Open up the butterfly and add the third paper clip over the taped-down ends of the first two. Tape it tightly in place with two pieces of tape.

12. Turn the glider over and bend up the back edges of its wings a little bit. If they are bent down, the glider will nose-dive.

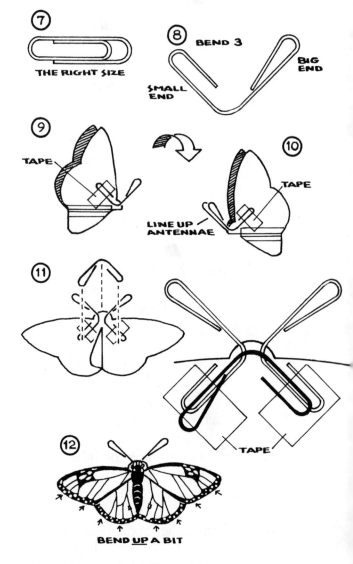

Flying Tips

• Before launching, look at the glider head-on from the front. The wings should be held up in a wide V with the keel straight down.

HEAD-ON FRONT VIEW KEEL

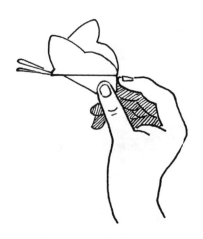

• To launch the glider, hold the keel between your thumb and middle finger with your first finger along its back edge. Then throw it as you would throw any glider.

- **Net Game:** As one or two kids throw Butterfly Gliders, another tries to catch the gliders with a real net. The catcher must stand twenty paces from the throwers. You get one point for each catch. Change catchers every ten throws.
- Outdoors, the glider will fly best on a calm day or on a day with a steady light breeze. Throw it upward fairly hard and into the face of an oncoming breeze.
- If the glider curves to one side again and again, there may be too much weight on the side it curves toward. Try bending the antennae a bit toward the opposite side. Experiment till you find the best position for them.

Fly-a-Fly Bug Glider

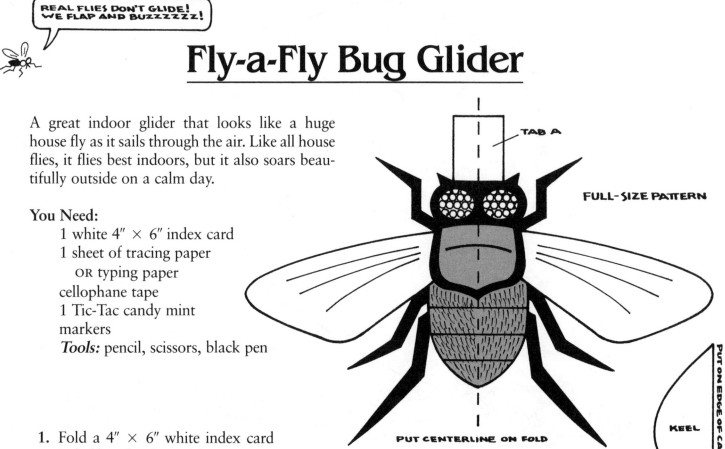

REAL FLIES DON'T GLIDE!
WE FLAP AND BUZZZZZZ!

TAB A

FULL-SIZE PATTERN

PUT ON EDGE OF CARD

KEEL

PUT CENTERLINE ON FOLD

A great indoor glider that looks like a huge house fly as it sails through the air. Like all house flies, it flies best indoors, but it also soars beautifully outside on a calm day.

You Need:
    1 white 4″ × 6″ index card
    1 sheet of tracing paper
      OR typing paper
    cellophane tape
    1 Tic-Tac candy mint
    markers
    Tools: pencil, scissors, black pen

1. Fold a 4″ × 6″ white index card in half so the short sides meet.

2. Copy the outline of half of the full-size pattern on this page onto the folded index card. (See page 8 for a simple way to do this.) Make sure the centerline of the pattern goes along the fold of the index card. The straight edge of the keel pattern can lie along any outside edge of the card.

3. Cut through both sides of the card at once along the outline to make the fly shape. For the keel, cut through only one side of the card.

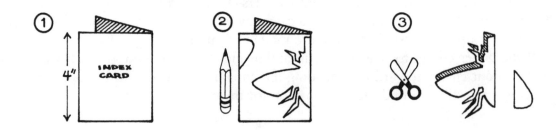

① INDEX CARD   4″

②

③

4. Leave the fly shape folded and lay it on a table. Lay the keel in place next to it with a tiny gap (¹⁄₁₆″) between them.

5. Tape the fly and the keel together.

6. Turn the fly over and tape the other side. Snip off corners of tape that stick out past the edges of the fly and the keel.

7. Open the wings and lay the fly on a table with the keel folded to one side under it. Decorate the up side with markers. Leave the wings white and add black lines. Make the head and legs black, the eyes red, and the body green. Draw little hairs all over the fly's abdomen and draw many tiny circles on the eyes to represent the many lenses of a fly's wonderful compound eyes.

8. Turn the fly over, keel side up, and fold Tab A up at a right angle.

9. A Tic-Tac candy mint is used as the weight to pull the glider forward through the air. Tape a Tic-Tac in the corner made by Tab A and the head of the fly.

10. Curve Tab A tightly around the Tic-Tac weight and tape it to the underside of the fly's head.

11. Bend the rear legs and the rear wing edges (shaded in Diagram 11) *up* slightly. If they are bent down, the glider will nose-dive.

See the next page for "Flying Tips."

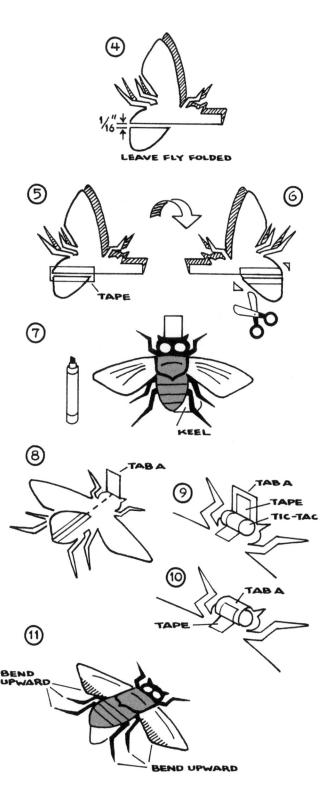

65

Flying Tips

- Before launching, look at the Fly-a-Fly Bug Glider head-on from the front. The wings should be held up in a wide V with the keel straight down.
- Like all house flies, this glider is happiest indoors. You can also fly it outdoors on a day with little or no breeze.
- To launch the glider, hold the keel between your thumb and middle finger with your first finger along its back edge. Then throw it as you would throw any glider.
- If the glider curves to one side again and again instead of flying straight, the keel is probably bent. Straighten and smooth it with your fingers. If that doesn't correct the curving, try shifting the Tic-Tac nose weight a little bit away from the side the glider curves toward.

KEEL

HEAD-ON FRONT VIEW

Dracula's Bat Kite

Every summer when Dracula was a kid his family went to the seacoast of Transylvania for a two-week vacation. Since he hated to lie around in the sun, Dracula spent his time flying his pet vampire bat on the end of a string. He attached a blood-red streamer to make his bat look like a kite, but not many people were fooled.

This construction-paper version of Dracula's Bat Kite is almost as realistic as his real bat. It flies high, and the red streamer shows off its graceful movements. The kite behaves so much like a bat that sometimes it darts forward as if it's snapping up insects in midair.

You Need:
    1 sheet of black construction paper
      (the lightweight kind that you buy
      in a 9″ × 12″ pad)
    1 sheet of tracing paper OR typing paper
    1 spool of black sewing thread
    1 toothpick (round OR flat)
    1 plastic soda straw
    cellophane tape
    2 sheets of red construction paper
    Tools: pencil, scissors, ruler, compass, black pen

TINY SAND BATS

1. Fold a piece of lightweight black construction paper in half so the short sides meet.

2. Find the full-size pattern on page 71. Page 8 shows you an easy way to copy it onto the construction paper. Be sure to put the straight centerline along the fold.

3. Cut through both sides of the paper at once along the outline.

① BLACK PAPER

②

③

4. With a compass point, make a small hole through the centerline of the bat at the exact point marked on the full-size pattern.

5. Black sewing thread is your kite-flying line. It's plenty strong enough for this small kite. The thread spool will be your kite-line reel. Pass the free end of your black thread through the hole you made in Step 4. Start from the side of the kite with the hill of the fold and push the thread through to the side with the valley of the fold.

6. Tie the thread tightly around a toothpick.

7. Pull the thread back through the hole till the toothpick lies snugly in the valley of the fold. Tape it in place with two pieces of tape.

8. Cut a plastic soda straw in half.

9. Lay the soda straw sections on the bat shape as shown. Notice that the straw sections make a line crossing the point where the thread is attached. Tape down the ends of the straw sections as shown. Snip off any tape that sticks out past the edges of the wings.

10. Pinch the free end of one soda straw section and push it into the open end of the other soda straw section. Push the straw sections together until the bat kite forms a wide V when you look at it head-on from the tips of the ears. This V shape makes the Bat Kite a steady flier.

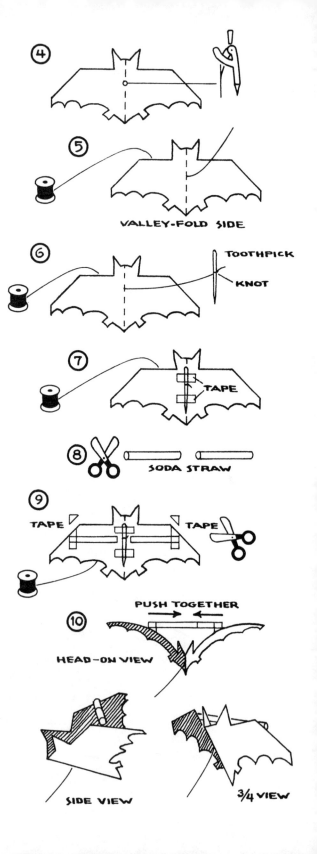

11. Now make a streamer tail. Cut two sheets of red construction paper into strips 1″ wide. Tape six strips together end to end. Tape one end of the tail inside the back tip of the bat shape. Save the extra strips for a windy day, when you may need an extra-long tail to keep the kite steady.

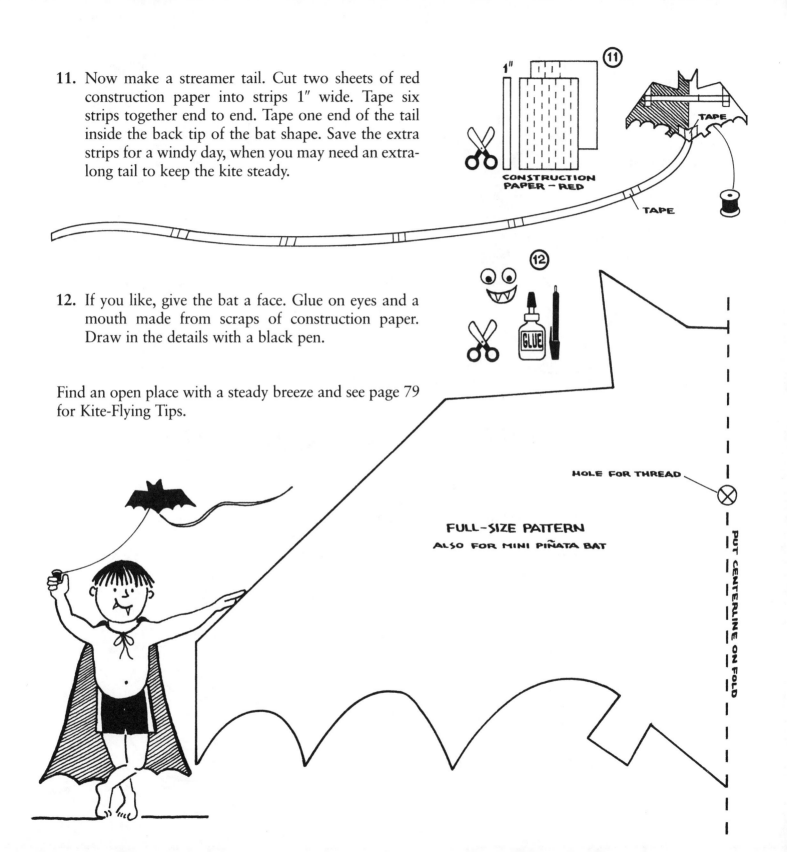

1″

CONSTRUCTION PAPER – RED

TAPE

TAPE

⑪

⑫

12. If you like, give the bat a face. Glue on eyes and a mouth made from scraps of construction paper. Draw in the details with a black pen.

GLUE

Find an open place with a steady breeze and see page 79 for Kite-Flying Tips.

HOLE FOR THREAD

FULL-SIZE PATTERN
ALSO FOR MINI PIÑATA BAT

PUT CENTERLINE ON FOLD

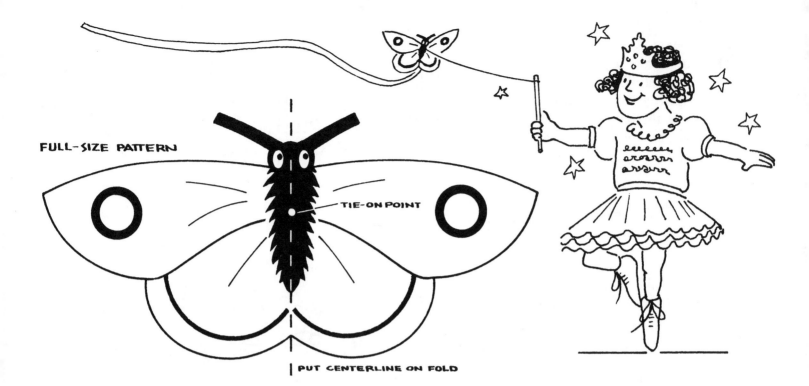

FULL-SIZE PATTERN

TIE-ON POINT

PUT CENTERLINE ON FOLD

Butterfly on a Magic Wand

Wave the wand and watch the little butterfly kite chase it through the air. Its flight is magical. Perfect for indoor flying because it can turn on a dime and circle as you spin with it.

Use it outdoors, too, but only on a day with NO breeze. Hold the wand up as you run and the butterfly will zip along after you. It's like having a pet butterfly on a leash.

You Need:
    1 piece of copy paper OR typing paper
    1 piece of tracing paper OR typing paper
    colored markers
    sewing thread
    1 toothpick (round or flat)
    cellophane tape
    1 soda straw
    Tools: scissors, compass, ruler

1. Fold a piece of copy paper in half.

2. Page 8 shows you an easy way to copy the full-size pattern on the facing page onto your paper. Copy the outline of only half the pattern. Make sure the centerline of the pattern lies along the fold of the paper. Mark the tie-on point.

3. Cut through both sides of the paper at once along the outline. Be careful cutting around the antennae. These antennae are much thicker than the ones on a real butterfly so they will hold up as the toy flies.

4. With the point of a compass, punch a small hole in the centerline of the butterfly at the tie-on point (¾″ from the top of its head).

5. With markers, decorate the side of the butterfly that has the hill of the fold.

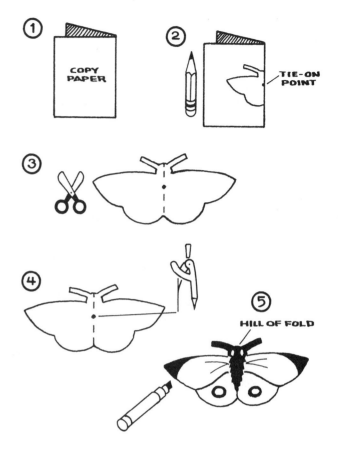

6. Cut a piece of sewing thread about 24″ long. Pass one end of it through the hole from the hill side of the fold to the valley side.

7. Break a toothpick in half. Tie the end of the thread tightly around it.

8. Pull the long end of the thread till the half toothpick rests snugly in the valley of the fold. Tape it in place.

9. Tie the free end of the thread to one end of the soda straw wand and tape it in place. Allow 16″ of thread between butterfly and wand.

10. Now for a streamer tail. Cut three strips of copy paper or typing paper, ¼″ × 11″ each.

11. Tape the strips together end to end and tape one end to the bottom of the butterfly in the valley of the fold.

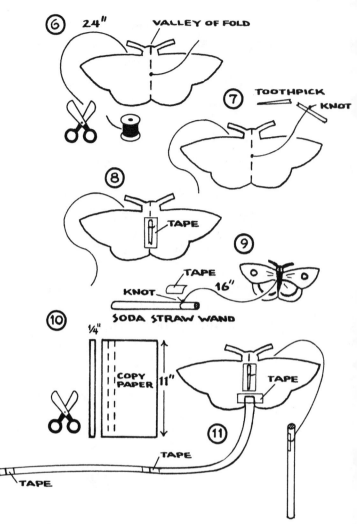

Flying Tips

- Be sure the butterfly's wings make a wide V when you look at them head-on from the front.
- This butterfly works best indoors.
- Hold the wand away from your body. Wave it round and round, back and forth, up and down, any way you like, and the butterfly will fly after it gracefully.
- It's fun to spin and get dizzy as the butterfly circles you.

If Kids Could Fly

If kids could fly like butterflies, this is how they might look. Butterflies do a lot of flapping as they fly. The fastest butterflies have narrow wings and flap more often than their wide-winged, slower-flying cousins. It's too bad kids' arms are just *too* narrow for any kind of flying — fast or slow. And kids are a little *heavy* for flying, too.

Easy Bug Kite

Easy to make. Easy to fly. You'll have this kite soaring in no time at all.

You Need:

    3 sheets of construction paper
      (the lightweight kind you buy
      in a 9″ × 12″ pad)
    1 sheet of tracing paper OR typing paper
    1 spool of sewing thread
    2 plastic soda straws
    cellophane tape
    black marker
    Tools: pencil, scissors, ruler,
      compass

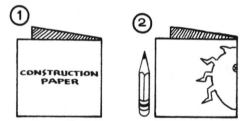

1. Fold a piece of lightweight construction paper in half so the short sides meet. Red is your color if you want a ladybug, but all the colors fly and look great in the sky.

2. Page 8 shows you an easy way to copy the full-size pattern on this page onto the construction paper. Be sure to put the straight edge of the pattern along the fold

HOLE FOR THREAD ⊗

PUT CENTERLINE ON FOLD

FULL-SIZE PATTERN

SODA STRAW

HILL-FOLD SIDE

VALLEY-FOLD SIDE

TAPE

3. Cut through both sides of the paper at once along the outline.

4. With a black marker, decorate the side of the bug with the hill of the fold. (The valley-fold side will be the back of the kite.) Make a ladybug — or use your imagination.

5. With a compass point, make a small hole through the centerline of the bug at the point marked on the full-size pattern.

6. Sewing thread is your kite-flying line. The thread spool will be your kite-line reel. Pass the free end of your thread through the hole you made in Step 5. Start from the side of the kite with the hill of the fold and push the thread through to the side with the valley of the fold.

7. Tie the thread tightly around a soda straw.

8. Pull the thread back through the hole till the straw lies snugly in the valley of the fold. Tape it in place with three pieces of tape. Snip off the end that sticks out past the edge of the bug.

9. Cut a 5½″ piece from a plastic soda straw.

10. Lay the 5½″ soda straw piece on the bug shape as shown. It crosses the first soda straw at the point where the thread is tied on. Tape down one end of the soda straw piece as shown.

11. Pull the free end of the soda straw piece to the other side of the bug shape and tape it in place as shown. This will give the bug a wide V shape when you look at it head-on from the top end. This V shape makes the Bug Kite a steady flier.

12. Now make a streamer tail. Cut two sheets of construction paper into strips 1″ wide (you pick the color). Tape six strips together end to end. Tape one end to the tail inside the back tip of the bug. Save the extra strips for a windy day, when you may need an extra-long tail to keep the kite steady.

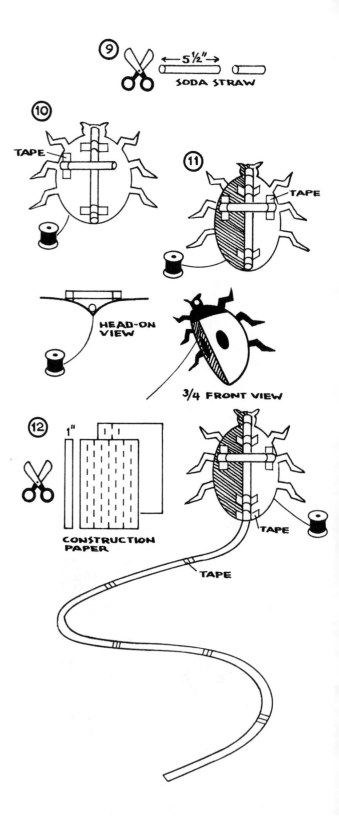

Kite-Flying Tips

For Dracula's Bat Kite (page 68) and
Easy Bug Kite (page 76)

Running with Kites

To fly a kite high overhead, you need special conditions — a wide-open place and the perfect breeze. But you can *run* with a small kite in almost any park or yard. Just keep the line short — two feet is plenty — so the kite can't catch in tree branches. And be sure to stay far away from overhead wires. You can run with a small kite on a day when there is absolutely no breeze, and it will bob up over your head and follow you through the air. If there is a breeze, run *toward* it so you feel it on your face. If there's a strong wind, wait for another day.

High Flying

- **Find the perfect place** with no wires overhead or trees to catch your kite, no roads or airports nearby, and no buildings to block the wind. Beaches and open fields are best.
- **Pick the perfect day** with a steady breeze or light wind. Days with strong winds and gusty breezes are not good for flying small kites.
- **Stand with your back to the wind.** If you have a good breeze, the Bug or the Bat should take off from your hands. Hold the thread spool in one hand and the kite in the other with a couple of feet of thread between them. Toss the kite gently up and away from you and tug back lightly on the thread to get the kite aloft. Now let out thread and the kite will fly out and away from you. Next, pull in on the thread and the kite will climb.
- **The wind is too strong** if the kite does a lot of crazy acrobatic looping. Reel the kite in and make the tail longer by taping on extra strips of paper. If that doesn't help, try again another day.
- **The breeze is too weak** if the kite won't rise. Make the tail shorter by taking away a couple of strips of paper. If that doesn't help, run toward the breeze and the kite will take off behind you. Let out thread as you run and your kite may climb up to a stronger overhead breeze that will hold it and give you a rest. Or you can just keep running.